PUFFIN BOOKS

FAME! WHO'S WHO IN HISTORY AT MADAME TUSSAUD'S

For some people, fame is short-lived; for others – just a few in each generation – it lasts for ever. Who could ever forget such names as William Shakespeare, Adolf Hitler, Jack the Ripper, William the Conqueror or, indeed, Madame Tussaud? And the names of Nelson Mandela, Margaret Thatcher and Mikhail Gorbachev are unlikely to be forgotten in the future. This is a book about famous people such as these. It will help you understand why they became famous (or infamous) and why they earned themselves a place in Madame Tussaud's. At the bottom of each page is a time-line which will help you find out what else was going on in the world when these people lived and how most of these events affect the way we live today.

So read on – who knows, maybe YOU could be on these pages in years to come!

Wendy Cooling lives in London and is head of The Children's Book Foundation. She was a teacher for many years and deputy head of a London comprehensive school. She has written several junior guides and topic packs for the National Trust. This is her first book for Puffin.

CW01067089

F A M E !
Who's Who
in History at Madame Tussaud's

Wendy Cooling

Illustrated by
Nick Duffy

PUFFIN BOOKS

PUFFIN BOOKS

Published by the Penguin Group
Penguin Books Ltd, 27 Wrights Lane, London W8 5TZ, England
Penguin Books USA Inc., 375 Hudson Street, New York, New York 10014, USA
Penguin Books Australia Ltd, Ringwood, Australia
Penguin Books Canada Ltd, 10 Alcorn Avenue, Toronto, Ontario, Canada M4V 3B2
Penguin Books (NZ) Ltd, 182–190 Wairau Road, Auckland 10, New Zealand

Penguin Books Ltd, Registered Offices: Harmondsworth, Middlesex, England

First published 1992
1 3 5 7 9 10 8 6 4 2

Text copyright © Wendy Cooling, 1992
Illustrations copyright © Nick Duffy, 1992
All rights reserved

The moral right of the author has been asserted

Printed in England by Clays Ltd, St Ives plc
Filmset in Rockwell Light

Contents

Introduction

How many of these names do you recognize?

Wilma Rudolph   Ernest Marples

Cliff Michelmore   George Brown

Pat Smythe   Frankie Vaughan

Lester Pearson   Leslie Caron

They were all to be seen in wax at Madame Tussaud's in 1964. They were famous politicians, sports personalities and stars of radio, TV and film at that time.

Today in their places stand, among others:

Ian Botham   Cher   Joan Collins

John Major   Nick Faldo   Pavarotti

In twenty-five years' time will the younger generation recognize these names? Some are already nearing the end of their careers and moving out of the public eye and soon new personalities will take their places. Fame, it seems, is often very short-lived.

For many people fame is transient, for others – just a few in every generation – it lasts for ever. It is unlikely that the names of Henry VIII, Adolf Hitler, Lenin, Guy Fawkes and Shakespeare will ever be forgotten. It is with these people that this book is mainly concerned. Who do you think will be the remembered names of your generation?

The waxwork figures in Madame Tussaud's exhibition, in London, reflect history, as well as the changes in our world and our society. The earliest figure is of William the Conqueror, who invaded England in 1066, perhaps the best-known date in British history. Not until Elizabeth I (1533–1603) does a woman appear in her own right. Before her came only the wives of Henry VIII, there because they married the king and because there were six of them! Today the halls of politicians, sportsmen and women and stars of stage and screen reflect the equality of all people. In our society it is possible for people from all walks of life to achieve fame, and Madame Tussaud's honours their success.

The people in this book are not necessarily the greatest figures in history, but for some reason the public are interested in them and still flock to see their likenesses in wax.

William the Conqueror (1027-1087)

William was the son of the Duke of Normandy and a servant girl. The Duke died when William was only eight years old, and from then on the boy's life was full of struggle and danger. William was a strong young man. He fought to be recognized as the Duke of Normandy, and soon no one dared disobey him. Why is this Frenchman so well remembered? Why is 1066, the date of his arrival in Britain, one of the most well-known dates in British history?

As William's strength in France grew, he began to think of taking power in England. Edward the Confessor, King of England, had no children and promised that William would be king when he died. Harold, an English earl, promised to support William's claim to the throne but, when Edward died, Harold became king and was crowned in Westminster Abbey. Duke William was angry and made plans to invade England. In 1066 his armies crossed the Channel and defeated Harold's army at the Battle of Hastings, where it is said that Harold was killed by an arrow which

1067 Building of Tower of London began

9

pierced his eye. On 25 December 1066, William was crowned King of England.

We know a great deal about William's famous battle because a wonderful tapestry was embroidered in honour of the Norman victory. The tapestry can still be seen in Bayeux, France. It is 70.4m long and 50.8cm high, and tells the story of the meeting in France between Harold and William, and of their battle at Hastings. It has helped historians to learn about the ships, clothes and weapons of the time, and to know something about the appearance of King William I of England, usually known as William the Conqueror.

The Norman Conquest was a turning point in British history. King William defeated those who fought against him and slowly brought order to what had been a troubled country. He planned the building of great castles, from which his soldiers could control the people and put down rebellions. Many of these castles still stand. Some, such as the one at Norwich, are now museums.

William is also remembered for ordering a survey of England known as the Domesday Book. In it are recorded the details of who lived where, who owned the land, what animals were kept and how much tax should be paid. It also recorded local customs, so it tells us a lot about life in Norman England.

William was a man who was feared rather than loved but, by the time he died, England was more peaceful and ordered than ever before. He had earned a lasting place in the history of England.

1086 Domesday Book completed

Richard the Lion Heart
(1157-1199)

Richard I of England, known as Richard the Lion Heart, was king for ten years, but spent only six months of that time in England. He was a great soldier, full of spirit and leadership, and was the only English king ever to take part in a Crusade to the Holy Land.

Richard was the eldest son of Henry II and promised loyalty to the King of France when his father died. Henry's wife, Eleanor of Aquitane, had turned his sons against him. The family was never united and Richard's brother John was always plotting against him. In 1190, when Richard had been king for only four months, he set out for the Holy Land to fight the Third Crusade. He was a tall, handsome man with reddish-brown hair, a powerful leader and a good soldier.

The Crusades, or Holy Wars, had started in 1095 when pilgrims to the holy places where Jesus lived and taught reported that they had been badly treated by the Turks who ruled in Palestine. This was unusual as the Turks were interested in learning and usually let people of other religions

---

1154 English man elected as Pope Adrian IV

worship freely. The Turks were Muslims, believers in the prophet Muhammad who was born in Mecca in about AD 570. Muhammad promised rewards in heaven for Muslims who fought for their faith. The Catholic Church encouraged the Crusaders to try to take Palestine from the Turks.

Saladin, Sultan of Egypt and Syria, fought in many battles and by 1187 had defeated the Christian armies and retaken Jerusalem, as well as most of the fortified places along the Syrian coast. This led a huge army of Crusaders, headed by the kings of France and England, to set off on the Third Crusade. They captured Acre in 1191, and Richard the Lion Heart defeated Saladin and took Caesarea and Jaffa, but never Jerusalem. Richard and Saladin held talks and seemed to respect each other. Permission was gained for Christian pilgrims to visit Jerusalem, but Richard saw the Crusade as a failure because the holy places remained in the hands of Muslims.

Richard returned to England for two months and then set off to fight the King of Spain. He was killed in the campaign and was buried in France. Richard was a fine soldier and a brave man, but he neglected his country for glory in distant wars.

1161 Chinese used explosives in warfare

King John
(1167-1216)

John was the youngest son of Henry II of England. He was not a very pleasant person and was cruel and aggressive. He was always plotting to take the throne from his brother, Richard the Lion Heart. Richard had been away fighting in the Crusades for most of his reign and his absence had weakened both England and the power of the Crown. There were constant disagreements, and even war, between the kings and princes of the British Isles, and between King John and the powerful landowners called barons. The wars had been very expensive and when John became king in 1199, he didn't have enough money to defend his lands in England and France. He was disliked by the people and soon the barons, supported by the Church, rebelled against him.

In 1215, John was forced to make peace with the barons and the Church. The barons met the king at Runnymede, an island on the River Thames near London, and forced him to seal the Magna Carta – the Great Charter. (At that time,

---

1167 Founding of Oxford University

seals were used on important documents instead of signatures.) The Magna Carta is important because it formed the beginnings of people's rights. When he put his seal on the Magna Carta, the king promised justice to all freemen – they could not be taxed without the consent of the Great Council, and could not be punished without trial. These rights were given only to freemen, not to the many serfs who worked for the lords and barons who owned the land. The charter was the foundation on which the ideas for individual rights were to be built. King John's reign was neither happy nor peaceful for England, and he is remembered not as a good king, but as the king who had to be forced to give rights to the people.

Four copies of the Magna Carta still exist – two of them are in the British Museum and the others in the cathedrals of Lincoln and Salisbury.

1206 Genghis Khan conquered Asia

Edward the Black Prince (1330-1376)

Edward was the eldest son of King Edward III; his father made him Prince of Wales when he was thirteen, and it was expected that he would be the next king of England. When the prince was only sixteen he fought the French at the Battle of Crécy, and helped his father to win a great victory. He was a fearless and impressive young man. He wore a suit of black armour when fighting which gave him his popular name – the Black Prince.

In 1349 the Black Death, a deadly plague, swept through Britain and a third of the population died. The loss of so many people made many changes necessary between masters and workers. During the reign of Edward III English became the official language, replacing French and Latin. Parliament was divided for the first time into an Upper and a Lower House – known today as the House of Lords and the House of Commons.

The Battle of Crécy was just the beginning of the Black Prince's career as a soldier. England was fighting the Hundred Years War against the

---

1333 Civil war in Japan

French, with areas of France being captured and lost. The close family relationship between the English and French royal families made Edward III claim that he was the rightful king of France. Most of the Prince of Wales's life was spent fighting in France – he was hated by the French for his ruthlessness and cruelty. Edward became worn out by battles and sickness, and returned home in 1371. He spent the rest of his life on a sick-bed. He died in 1376, a few months before his father, and so never became king.

In 1361 the Black Prince had married his cousin, Joan the Fair Maid of Kent, and they had two sons, Edward and Richard. Richard became King Richard II a year after his father's death and, in 1396, he ended the long war against France.

1350 English replaced French in England's schools

King Henry V
(1387-1422)

Like many of England's early kings, Henry V is remembered because he was a brave soldier who led his armies to victory against the French. Unlike some of the former kings, he was loved by his people and is also remembered as a fair and honest ruler.

England was at war with France and, in 1415, Henry V went to Normandy to fight for the Crown of France. He led his armies to great victory at Harfleur and at Agincourt. In the Battle of Agincourt, the huge French army charged head-on into the smaller English army, which was suffering from hunger and sickness – 7000 Frenchmen and 400 Englishmen died. The English victory led to a treaty which declared that Henry should marry Princess Katherine, the daughter of the King of France, and that any son they had should rule both England and France. Henry V died soon after, on yet another campaign, leaving his baby son, Henry VI, to become king.

According to Shakespeare's play, *Henry the Fifth*, Henry had been a wild boy in his youth

---

1388 Chaucer wrote the *Canterbury Tales*

when he was known as Prince Hal. It is perhaps because of the play that Henry V is so well remembered. Shakespeare described him as a lively, hard-drinking young man, enjoying life with his large friend Falstaff, but changing when he became king and immediately taking his responsibilities seriously. The king in Shakespeare's play makes a famous speech to his men before the battle of Harfleur. It begins:

> Once more unto the breach, dear
>   friends, once more;
> Or close the wall up with our English
>   dead.
> In peace there's nothing so becomes a
>   man
> As modest stillness and humility;
> But when the blast of war blows in our
>   ears,
> Then imitate the actions of a tiger . . .

and ends with the rousing *'Cry God for Harry, England and Saint George!'* A good ending as the English soldiers went into battle wearing the cross of Saint George, England's patron saint. Just before the Battle of Agincourt, Henry dresses as a common soldier and walks unrecognized among his men. Then in perhaps the most memorable speech of the play he speaks to his army on the eve of battle, telling them to leave if they do not fully support him. The speech ends:

> . . . *he to-day that sheds his blood with me*
>   *Shall be my brother . . .*

1408 Donatello finished statue of David

And gentlemen in England now a-bed
Shall think themselves accurs'd they
* were not here,*
And hold their manhoods cheap whiles
* any speaks*
Who fought with us upon Saint Crispin's
* day.*

Henry V, the great leader, led his men to victory.
It is probably because of the words Shakespeare
put into the king's mouth that we remember this.

1412 Birth of Joan of Arc

Henry VIII
(1491-1547)

Henry VIII, the second of the Tudor kings, is one of England's best-remembered monarchs – why?

Because of his break with the Church of Rome and founding of the Church of England?

Because of his portly, elaborately dressed figure?

Because of his famous Holbein portrait?

Because of his good education?

Because of his strong rule?

No! Henry VIII is remembered first as the king who had six wives, six wives at a time when divorce was almost unheard of! As king, he could get rid of his wives when they no longer pleased him. He broke with the Church of Rome in order to divorce his first wife and later ordered the beheading of two of his wives, claiming they were unfaithful.

Henry lived during the Renaissance, a time of great change in Europe, when there was a rebirth of interest in learning and the arts. The printing press had come to England from Germany and

---

1492 Columbus landed on San Salvador

---

had made it possible to produce books more cheaply and quickly – before this books had been written by hand, usually by monks. More books meant further spreading of new ideas. When Henry was still a baby, Christopher Columbus had sailed to the American continent and, during Henry's lifetime, other great adventurers were making voyages, reaching distant lands and learning more about the world.

Henry was given a good education. He was well read and he learnt Latin, Spanish, Italian and French. He could play the lute and the harp. He was a horseman, a good archer and a tennis player. He enjoyed talking to scholars, like Sir Thomas More, and discussing all that was new.

Henry was a ruler who would do anything to get what he wanted and to remain all-powerful. His word was law and he ordered the deaths of those who disagreed with him. Even his former friend, Sir Thomas More, was sent to the scaffold because he refused to agree that Henry, and not the Pope, was head of the Church of England. No one could safely defy him, but his absolute power gave England a time of relative peace and prosperity.

1492 Leonardo da Vinci designed a flying-machine

Henry VIII's Wives

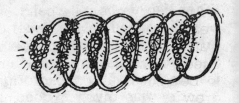

The most powerful countries in Europe in the sixteenth century were France and Spain. To ensure peace with Spain, Henry VII had arranged for Arthur, his eldest son, to marry the Spanish princess, Catherine of Aragon. Arthur was fifteen when he married Catherine, and she was sixteen. The following year Arthur died and Henry, the king's second son, became heir to the throne, and on the death of Henry VII he became King Henry VIII of England. Henry then married Catherine, his brother's widow. This marriage was against the rules of the Church, but the Pope was finally persuaded to give his blessing. Henry and Catherine had one child, Princess Mary.

Henry desperately wanted to have a son. He decided to divorce Catherine and marry a younger woman. He sent his close adviser, Cardinal Wolsey, to Rome to ask the Pope for a divorce from Catherine. The Pope was very angry because he had been very reluctant to agree to Henry and Catherine's marriage in the first place. Henry was determined to marry Anne Boleyn, and after six years of talks with the Pope, he too

---

1517 Martin Luther protested against Catholicism

22

was angry. He blamed Wolsey for the Pope's refusal to grant a divorce, broke with the Church of Rome, declared himself head of the Church of England and immediately married Anne Boleyn.

Anne Boleyn was a maid of honour; she was wealthy and well educated. Once she realized that the king liked her, she set out to become queen. Anne and Henry had a daughter, who was to become Elizabeth I of England. Soon Henry grew tired of Anne and wanted to marry Jane Seymour. He knew the English people would not like another divorce, so he accused Anne of being unfaithful – she was condemned and beheaded. She had been queen for only three years.

Jane Seymour was said to be pretty but not very bright. Henry married her in 1536, on the day after Anne Boleyn's execution. Some say that Jane was the only wife that Henry really loved. She was queen for only a year and died a few days after giving birth to the son Henry so desperately wanted. Her son became King Edward VI of England.

In 1540 Henry married Anne of Cleves. This was a political marriage made to gain Germany's support for England. Henry was shown a portrait of Anne and thought she looked beautiful, but when he saw her he was angry to find that she was nothing like her picture: she was very plain, even ugly. He had to marry her because the agreement had been made; he called her a 'great Flanders mare' and they were soon separated. Henry divorced her and this time it was Thomas Cromwell, having arranged the marriage, who was charged with treason and executed.

1519 Birth of the Sikh religion

Catherine Howard was Henry's fifth wife, and she too didn't live to enjoy being Queen of England for long. Henry was now nearly fifty, he had lost his attractiveness, and was getting fat and bad-tempered. Catherine was a spoilt young woman and liked being admired by men, and she continued to meet her old flames after her marriage. She married Henry in 1540, in 1541 she was imprisoned in the Tower of London accused of adultery, and in 1542 she was beheaded.

Henry was not keen to marry again, but seemed to need a companion. In 1543 he married Catherine Parr, who was lucky enough to outlive her much-married husband.

1526 Koh-i-noor diamond taken from Agra

Queen Elizabeth I
(1533-1603)

Anne Boleyn, Henry VIII's second wife, was Queen of England for only three years but her daughter, Elizabeth, became one of England's best-loved and best-remembered rulers – she was queen for forty-five years. Her reign was a time of great voyages, adventure, war with Spain, an age of poetry and of plays. Elizabeth never married, but she had her favourites among the noblemen of England. When her sister, Queen Mary, died, England was a poor country, but by the end of Elizabeth's reign it was rich and prosperous, one of the greatest countries in Europe. Women, however, were seen as less strong, less important and less intelligent than men. Queen Elizabeth, in a speech to her soldiers as the Spanish Armada sailed to attack England, showed her great strength as she said:

> 'I know I have but the body of a weak and feeble woman; but I have the heart and stomach ... of a King of England, too; and I think foul scorn that ... Spain,

---

1534 Anglican Church founded

25

or any Prince of Europe, should dare to invade the borders of my realms. I myself will be your general, and I doubt not we shall shortly have a famous victory over the enemies of my God, of my kingdom, and of my people.'

Elizabeth did not have a happy childhood. Her parents were disappointed by her birth as they had desperately wanted a boy. Her mother was executed when Elizabeth was still very young and her elder sister, Mary, was always afraid that Elizabeth would steal her throne. Mary became queen of England when Elizabeth was twenty, and soon believed that her sister was plotting against her. Elizabeth was arrested and imprisoned in the Tower of London, a very grim place. Later she was confined at Hatfield House, where she spent her time learning Latin and Greek, and became a good scholar. Mary was always angry with her young half-sister because Elizabeth was a Protestant and Mary was a very devout Catholic. When Mary died, the twenty-five-year-old Elizabeth became queen. She returned to London and was met by cheering crowds; the people were pleased to have a beautiful young queen.

Her cousin, also called Mary, was Queen of Scotland, and she tried to claim the English throne. For many years there were troubles between Elizabeth and Mary. After being a prisoner for twenty years, Mary became involved in a plot to kill Elizabeth. She was caught and beheaded.

Elizabeth was a flamboyant queen. She dressed in magnificent gowns and wore wonderful jewels.

1539 Bassoon invented in Italy

She can be seen in Madame Tussaud's in London wearing a perfect copy of a dress she wore to sit for a portrait; a beautiful dress of rich materials, decorated with lace, embroidery and jewels. She loved to travel around the country, and people always gathered to cheer and admire her. Elizabeth loved the plays of William Shakespeare and often ordered his company of actors to perform at the palace. She encouraged her sailors to find new lands and even sent a nobleman to the Court of the Mogul in Delhi, to arrange for trade between England and India.

Elizabeth was a strong queen and she never gave in. It is said that when she was dying, the King of Scotland, heir to the English throne, sent one of his men to see how ill she was. Elizabeth could hardly stand, but she got up, dressed in her most elaborate clothes and danced in front of the visitor. A few days later she died. James VI of Scotland became King James I of England – for the first time England and Scotland had the same king.

1547 Nostradamus began making predictions

Sir Francis Drake
(1540-1596)

Sir Francis Drake was one of the most famous of the Elizabethan sea-dogs: he was an adventurer, even a pirate, who sailed to distant lands and brought back great riches.

Until the sixteenth century, it was still believed by many that the world was saucer-shaped and that a ship sailing too far would go over the edge and be lost for ever. Explorers from Spain and Portugal disproved this by finding routes round the world, which increased the wealth and power of their countries. In the middle of the sixteenth century, the English joined in the race to find new trade routes and to claim new lands.

Francis Drake commanded his first ship when he was twenty-two, and soon became involved in the slave trade. Later he received Queen Elizabeth I's privateering commission and, in 1572, set off for the Spanish Main on a voyage of plunder. In 1577 he went on a long expedition to America, through the Straits of Magellan, and back to Europe through the Indian Ocean and round southern Africa – this was only the second ever

---

1547 Ivan the Terrible became Tsar of Russia

28

voyage round the world. On his return the queen met him on board his ship, the *Golden Hind*, and dubbed him a knight. He gave her the most precious of the jewels he had plundered.

The voyage had been hard – they had sailed through fifty-two days of storms as they entered the Pacific Ocean. Voyages were very long and conditions on ships were bad: accommodation was crowded and dirty, and food often ran out. Because there were no fresh vegetables many men died of scurvy, described thus in a book written at the time: 'Their gums waxe [grow] great, and swell, and they are fain to cut them away. Their legs swell and all the body becometh sore, and so benumbed that they cannot stir hand nor foot.' Sometimes as many as half the ship's crew died of the disease.

Discipline was harsh on board: punishments included flogging, ducking, being put in irons and keelhauling – where the man was dragged under water beneath the length of the whole ship. In spite of the risks and hardships, sailors went on voyages hoping for big rewards, for silks, spices, gold and jewels that would make them rich men.

Drake also achieved fame in the wars against Spain. In 1587, when the Spanish Armada was preparing to sail against England, Drake carried out a raid on the ships in Cadiz harbour, burning them and delaying the sailing date by a year; he called the raid 'the singeing of the King of Spain's beard'. When the Armada was finally sighted off Plymouth, Drake is said to have delayed boarding his ship in order to finish a game of bowls saying,

---

1564 Horse-drawn coach introduced to England

'There's plenty of time to win this game and to thrash the Spaniards too.'

Sir Francis Drake, like so many of his crew, succumbed to the terrible conditions on board ship – he died of dysentery in 1596, during a voyage to the West Indies.

William Shakespeare
(1564-1616)

William Shakespeare wrote plays, and acted in them, 400 years ago. The people who lived then, the Elizabethans and Jacobeans, loved his plays and today, all over the world, audiences still flock to see them. As Ben Jonson, one of Shakespeare's rivals, said: 'He was not for an age but for all time'. The facts about Shakespeare's life are not clear because he left no letters or diaries. We do know that he left his wife and children in Stratford-upon-Avon and went to London, joined an acting company and became a playwright.

The theatre was very exciting in Shakespeare's day and performances were very noisy and lively – booing and hissing as well as clapping were quite normal. There would be chatting during the play, even gambling, and sellers of food and drink would pass through the crowded audience throughout the performance. The stage was in the open air and the crowds bought seats in the three galleries that looked down on it and on the open yard where the 'groundlings', usually

---

1587 Monteverdi's book of madrigals published

poorer people, could stand and watch the play for one penny.

Shakespeare wrote his plays to suit his audiences – they loved plays about the history of England. These histories are still performed today – *Henry V* and *Richard III*, for example, have been made into films and so have been seen by millions of people. More light-hearted plays such as *A Midsummer Night's Dream* and *As You Like It* still delight audiences with their imagination, love, jokes and disguises. Perhaps the greatest are the famous tragedy plays such as *Hamlet, Macbeth, Othello* and *King Lear*: they have been performed in many different ways, and their themes and ideas are still of interest today.

Shakespeare returned to his family in Stratford-upon-Avon for his final years, and is buried there. On his tombstone are carved the words:

> *Good friend, for Jesus' sake forbear*
> *To dig the dust enclosed here;*
> *Blest be the man that spares these*
> * stones,*
> *And curst be he that moves my bones.*

1589 First water closet designed in England

Guy Fawkes
(1570-1606)

The name of Guy Fawkes is very well known in Britain, especially by children who celebrate his day every year on 5 November. It is a time of excitement, parties, fireworks and bonfires on which effigies of Guy Fawkes are burnt. After 400 years, why do we still remember the name of Guy Fawkes in this way? Why is he so infamous that his effigy is made and burnt by countless people?

Queen Elizabeth I had died in 1603, after ruling for forty-five years, and her cousin, James VI of Scotland, had become James I of England. It seemed to be the start of a new age, but once again religion was causing arguments. The English Catholics had supported James in his claim to the throne and although he was a Protestant, and head of the Church of England, they expected help from him in return. Being a Catholic was forbidden and anyone not attending a Church of England service on a Sunday could be fined a shilling. But the Roman Catholic religion survived in England, especially among those rich enough

---

1592 Ruins of Pompeii discovered

to pay their weekly fine. Once he became king, James had no time for the Catholics. This made them angry and two of them, Thomas Percy and Robert Catesby, decided to blow up the Houses of Parliament on 5 November 1605 at the State Opening, which the king always attended. Soon others, including Guy Fawkes, were brought into the plot.

A tunnel was started under the House of Lords, but as the date of the opening of Parliament grew nearer, the plotters had to rent a cellar which actually ran under the House. They moved in thirty-six barrels of gunpowder and loads of firewood. They waited for Parliament to meet, planning to strike a match at the right moment and send the Lords, and the king, up in flames.

Some of the plotters began to have doubts because there would also be some Catholics in the House as well as Protestants. One wrote a letter to a friend, advising him not to attend the opening ceremony. Suspicion was aroused and the letter was shown to the king. A thorough search was ordered and the gunpowder was discovered, along with Guy Fawkes, whose turn it was to be on guard.

Guy Fawkes was arrested and, under torture, told the names of the other plotters. They were all arrested, tried for high treason, found guilty, and hung, drawn and quartered. As a result, Catholics became even less popular in England.

Is it fair? Guy Fawkes is burnt every year, but how many people even remember the names of Percy and Catesby who planned and organized the whole affair?

1593 Plague closed London's theatres

Oliver Cromwell
(1599-1658)

Oliver Cromwell became a Member of Parliament in 1626 when Charles I was King of England. Charles thought that kings were made by God and that he should be allowed to rule as he wished. He ignored the advice of Parliament if he didn't like it. Charles had stormy relationships with all his Parliaments and, in 1642, the people of England were involved in a harsh civil war in which the king's supporters fought against Parliament's supporters.

Cromwell became a soldier and a general on the side of Parliament, and led his soldiers, known as the 'Ironsides', to great victories. His men never lost a battle and finally defeated the king at the Battle of Marston Moor, near York. After another victory at Naseby in Northamptonshire, Cromwell marched to London, where he was greeted as a great leader. He had no training as a soldier, but believed that men who had God on their side would succeed. He insisted on enthusiasm, discipline, and a belief in God and the cause. These principles produced an unbeatable army.

1620 The *Mayflower* sailed to the New World

Charles I was imprisoned on the Isle of Wight, but he continued to try to make a deal with Parliament. The years of civil war had been hard and soon the people were calling for the king's death. Charles was 'put on trial for his life. Cromwell didn't like the idea of killing a king, but came to believe that the many deaths in the civil war were the king's fault. In 1649 Oliver Cromwell signed the king's death warrant, Charles I was executed, and England became a republic.

Cromwell became a powerful leader and was soon made Lord Protector. He too argued with Parliament and, although he wanted to work with it, constant plots and conflicts made this almost impossible. Many of the quarrels with the king had been about religion and these arguments continued. Oliver Cromwell, unlike many Puritans, thought that people should be able to worship God in their own way. Both Catholic and Church of England services were held in peace and, after a gap of hundreds of years, Jews were once more allowed to settle and worship in England. Cromwell didn't really want to rule by force, but he lived in troubled times and nothing else seemed to work. He crushed the Irish revolt cruelly, putting many people to death and turning many more out of their homes and lands.

Oliver Cromwell was a great general and statesman, but his ambition and cruelty are also remembered. He died still believing that God and justice were on his side. He was given a splendid funeral at Westminster, but when Charles II became king, Cromwell's body was put on a gibbet at Tyburn and was then buried as a common criminal.

1650 Tea first drunk in England

Marie Antoinette
(1755-1793)

Marie Antoinette is best known as the queen who, when told that her people had no bread, is reputed to have said: *'Qu'ils mangent de la brioche'* – 'Let them eat cake'! We don't know if this is true but we do know that Madame Tussaud, who was in France at the time of the revolution, made a death-mask of Marie Antoinette. This can be seen in the Chamber of Horrors at Madame Tussaud's, next to the very guillotine blade that beheaded her in 1793.

Marie Antoinette was the daughter of Emperor Francis I and Maria Theresa of Austria. At fifteen she married the Dauphin of France, the heir to the French throne. When she was nineteen, her husband became King Louis XVI and she became queen of France. France was experiencing a time of great hardship and the people were discontented. They soon disliked the young queen who was extravagant and seemed unconcerned about their miseries. Her reputation grew worse when she obtained a diamond necklace worth £80,000 without paying for it. An admirer had

---

1759 Handel died and Hadyn wrote his first symphony

helped her to get the necklace and, when the jeweller sued for his money, the queen denied all knowledge of the affair. Her admirer was arrested, but the people were sure that it was Marie Antoinette who was guilty.

The queen didn't seem to understand that France's problems were serious. She opposed new ideas, she interfered in her husband's work and policy-making, and she probably speeded up the end of the monarchy in France. She did show great courage during the revolution but was too independent to take advice, or to accept changes, and to the last she failed to understand the times she lived in.

As conditions in Paris worsened, Marie Antoinette persuaded her husband that the family should escape from Paris and seek help from a sympathetic army commander – she also hoped that her Austrian relations would assist. On the night of 20 June 1791, Count Ferson, another of the queen's admirers, smuggled the royal family out of Paris. Unfortunately, Louis was recognized before they reached the frontier, and they were brought back to Paris under heavy guard. The attempted escape turned the people further against the king and demands to declare France a republic became stronger. The revolution grew in power and in January 1793, King Louis XVI was tried and executed. In August of the same year, after a period of imprisonment, Marie Antoinette was tried for treason and sentenced to death by the Revolutionary Tribunal. She went to her death at the guillotine with dignity and resignation.

1764 James Hargreaves invented the spinning-jenny

Wolfgang Amadeus Mozart
(1756-1791)

The young Mozart amazed the people of Salzburg in Austria by being able to play the harpsichord when he was three years old, and to write pieces of music when he was only five. He was what we call a child prodigy; his musical skills were extraordinary for such a young child. In his early years, his father took him on a concert tour of Europe and he performed for, and met, the famous people of the time, such as Queen Marie Antoinette of France and King George III of England.

Mozart went on to study in Italy and then returned to Austria, this time to Vienna, a city famous for its music. Despite his talent, Mozart's life was not easy. He couldn't write beautiful music unless he had money to live on. Because he was difficult to get on with, he found it hard to find rich patrons to support him.

His wife, Constanze, was charming but she was not a good manager, and they were always in debt. Their problems increased, even though Mozart was writing some of his greatest operas.

1769 James Watt patented his steam engine

Don Giovanni was such a success that Joseph II of Austria appointed Mozart as court musician and composer – his salary was eighty pounds a year! Mozart was no good with money, and when Constanze was ill he had to beg for help from his friends in order to care for her. He lived a fast life and when he was composing he worked hard, often staying up through the night and drinking a great deal to help him keep awake. Soon his health began to suffer, but he was unable to slow down and care for himself. He started to write a Requiem Mass – a special choral church service for the repose of the souls of the dead. Mozart seemed determined to complete this piece; it was as if he was writing his own requiem. Just before it was finished he caught typhoid and died, alone and in terrible poverty. He was only thirty-five years old. He was given a pauper's funeral and was buried in common ground. No one was ever able to find his grave.

Mozart gave the world music that is some of the greatest ever written. His symphonies, piano concertos and sonatas are still played regularly, and his operas continue to be staged all over the world. His music brought him little success in his lifetime, but soon after his death he was recognized as a great musical genius.

William Wilberforce (1759-1833)

After the voyages of the great explorers such as Columbus and Magellan, Europeans began to settle in the lands they found. The British settled in the islands of the Caribbean – the West Indies – and in America. They wanted to make money out of the new colonies, so they started huge plantations to grow sugar and cotton, crops that did well in a hot climate. The European settlers didn't want to work on the land and so they began to buy black slaves from West Africa to work for them. The slaves were kidnapped and sold in their own countries for goods such as guns, beads and gin. They were packed into airless holds below the ships' decks for the long voyage across the Atlantic Ocean. Many died on the journey and the slave-traders were happy if half their human cargo reached their destination.

In the slave markets, families were broken up as husbands, wives and children were often bought by different masters. The slaves had no rights on the plantations and were often worked to death by their owners – it was easy to get new

---

1773 The Boston Tea Party

slaves from Africa to replace them. By the end of the eighteenth century, when England had already been involved in the slave-trade for almost one hundred years, a few people began to think that slavery was evil and to speak out against it. William Wilberforce, a very religious man from Yorkshire, took up the fight to ban slavery. He was a young Member of Parliament and a friend of the Prime Minister, William Pitt. It should have been easy to stop the buying and selling of human beings, but it was not. Many people had grown rich through slavery and didn't want it stopped. But slowly, more and more people supported Wilberforce and, once, when he was too ill to make his speech against slavery in Parliament, the Prime Minister spoke in his place. Still Parliament voted to continue slavery. Wilberforce knew he needed to gain support, so he started to hold huge public meetings to tell the terrible stories about the lives of the slaves. For years he continued to argue his case in Parliament.

In 1807 Parliament passed a bill forbidding British shipowners to carry slaves from Africa. Still the trade went on – slaves were bought from foreign traders instead of from the British. Wilberforce battled on to make it illegal to own slaves and to set all slaves free. Finally, in 1833, just after Wilberforce died, a law was passed to ban slavery in all British-ruled lands.

William Wilberforce had given up his chance to be a great statesman, perhaps even prime minister, because he felt the fight against slavery was more important than anything else.

1776 American independence declared

Madame Tussaud
(1761-1850)

Madame Tussaud was born in Strasbourg, France and was christened Anna Maria Grosholtz. Her father, a soldier, died before she was born and Madame Grosholtz went with her daughter to be housekeeper for a Dr Curtius. The name Madame Tussaud is now known all over the world; she achieved amazing success, as an artist and business woman, in an age when women were not expected to have careers. She survived and succeeded in violent times and was clearly a most extraordinary woman.

Dr Curtius, whom she called uncle, was a modeller in wax and he was soon invited to establish a wax museum in Paris, which opened in 1770. Marie, as she was known, and her mother accompanied him to Paris. As Marie grew up she showed great power of observation and flair for model-making. Dr Curtius began to teach her his skills. At his exhibition, *Salon de Cire*, she met famous people who came to be modelled. Madame Elizabeth, King Louis XVI's sister, was impressed by her talent and she was invited to

---

1783 First manned flight in a hot-air balloon

43

the Palace of Versailles to teach the princess art. For nine years she lived with the French royal family.

France was changing; the hungry and the unemployed were angry at the way the rich lived and began to talk of revolution. Dr Curtius called her back to Paris at the outbreak of the French Revolution in 1789. There she lived through the frightening period of the Revolution: the storming of the Bastille and the beheading of many people, including King Louis XVI and Queen Marie Antoinette. Marie Grosholtz was forced to make death-masks of their heads as they fell from the guillotine – these models can still be seen at Madame Tussaud's. Many died on the guillotine and soon Marie and her mother were arrested too. They had, after all, been close to the royal family. They were taken to prison and shared a cell with nineteen other women; they slept on dirty straw and had their hair cut ready for the guillotine. After a week they were freed without explanation, and soon afterwards the revolution ended.

In 1793 Jean Paul Marat, a revolutionary politian, was stabbed to death in his bath. Marie was called to do a cast of him. She wrote: 'They came for me to go to Marat's house at once, and to take with me what appliances I needed to make an impression of his features. The cadaverous aspect of the fiend made me feel desperately ill, but they stood over me and forced me to perform the task.' In 1794 Dr Curtius died, leaving everything to Marie. She soon learned to run the exhibition, creating models as new public figures emerged. Marie married François Tussaud in 1795 but,

---

1785 Cartright patented the power loom

---

despite having a husband and two sons, her career always came first. She modelled the new leaders of France, including Napoleon, whose wife, Josephine, she had met in prison.

In 1802 Madame Tussaud's exhibition was only moderately successful in Paris and she decided to move to London. She never saw her husband again. Her wax exhibition was an immediate success and she began to model members of the British royal family. The exhibition toured the country for thirty-three years and there were always crowds of visitors. During this time, the Separate Room was introduced and it was described as being 'inadvisable for ladies to visit'. In 1846 the magazine *Punch* called it the Chamber of Horrors.

Today the Chamber of Horrors still fascinates and shocks visitors. The guillotine and the heads of the French king and queen, and the model of Marat dead in his bath, can be seen alongside modern murderers.

In 1835 Madame Tussaud, aged seventy-four, had tired of travelling and set up her permanent exhibition in Baker Street, London and in the following year she modelled Princess Victoria. Marie's sons were now also skilled artists, but she was still in charge. In 1837, when Victoria became queen, a coronation scene was made, followed by a wedding scene when Victoria married Albert in 1840. Not long after that, Marie handed the business over to her sons. She died in 1850, in her ninetieth year.

The exhibition, which has been in London's Marylebone Road since 1884, still bears her

---

1788 *The Times* newspaper began

name, and her traditions of accuracy and of being up to date continue to be honoured. Today it costs about £20,000 to make a model and those who are chosen to be modelled see it as an honour, and recognition of their fame.

Over two million people visit Madame Tussaud's every year and her name will live on for ever.

1789 William Blake wrote his Songs of Innocence

Napoleon
(1769-1821)

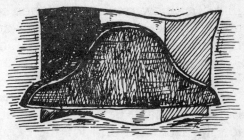

Napoleon was a great French soldier. He started his training when he was only ten years old, and became an officer in the French army when he was fifteen!

France was in turmoil after the 1789 Revolution. The king and queen, Louis XVI and Marie Antoinette, had been beheaded on the guillotine and the country had become a republic. The new leaders quarrelled with each other, and the surrounding countries were afraid that France's troubles might spread to them. They attacked France to stop this, but Napoleon led the French against the attacking armies and won great victories.

Napoleon was unusually short – only five feet two inches tall. We know exactly what Napoleon looked like because Madame Tussaud was a friend of his wife, Josephine. Madame Tussaud had befriended Josephine when they were both imprisoned during the revolution. Josephine arranged for her to have a sitting with Napoleon, and the model on view in London was taken from a life-cast made in Paris in 1801.

1812 Jewish quarters established in Morocco

Soon Napoleon's men were ready to follow him anywhere and they called him 'the little corporal'. The French saw him as their hero and the rest of Europe was terrified of him and his great army. In 1797 a new government was set up in France and Napoleon became its leader. In 1804 he became Emperor of France. The old rules of France had gone with the revolution and Napoleon worked hard to introduce new ones. The 'Code Napoléon' declared everyone equal before the law. Before, there had been one law for the rich and one for the poor. The new law was introduced in France and all the countries Napoleon conquered. The modern laws of much of Europe are based on the Code Napoléon.

Napoleon was successful for a time but he became too ambitious. He wanted more power: he wanted to rule Europe and he wanted to defeat the English army led by the Duke of Wellington, a great British general. In 1811 Napoleon marched into Russia and entered Moscow but, when he got caught up in the horrors of a freezing Russian winter, he was forced to retreat with his army. The departure of Napoleon from Russia is celebrated in a famous piece of music, the 1812 Overture, by the Russian composer Tchaikovsky.

The final defeat came to Napoleon when he met Wellington's army at the Battle of Waterloo in 1815. Napoleon fled to Paris, abdicated as Emperor and was banished to the Atlantic island of St Helena, where he died in lonely isolation six years later. In 1840 his body was taken back to Paris to the crypt of the Hôtel des Invalides.

1815 Battle of New Orleans

Ludwig van Beethoven
(1770-1827)

When Ludwig van Beethoven was only six he played the piano and violin far better than most adults. He worked hard, was always keen to learn and his musical talent grew to make him a lasting name as one of the world's greatest composers.

Ludwig did not have a happy childhood. He grew up in Bonn, in Germany, with his two brothers, his sister and his loving mother, Maria Magdalena, in a house ruled by a stern father who drank too much. Ludwig's father was a musician and soon saw the greatness of his son's musical ability. He thought there was money to be made out of this great talent and pushed the boy hard. Sometimes, coming in after a night's drinking, he would drag Ludwig from his bed and give him a music lesson, and there was trouble when Ludwig, still half asleep, made mistakes. The boy grew up terrified of his father. Luckily Ludwig was seen performing by the Court organist and was taken on as his pupil. His talents began to develop and his period of composing began.

1818 Mary Shelley's *Frankenstein* published

When he was seventeen Ludwig visited Vienna, where he met Mozart, who appreciated his musical talents. Soon after, his mother died and he returned to Bonn to take charge of the family.

At twenty-two Beethoven returned to Vienna and studied with Joseph Haydn, the greatest musician of the time. By now he was a brilliant pianist and was composing more of his own music. Soon the rich people of Vienna wanted to hear him play and students wanted to learn from him. Ludwig van Beethoven seemed to have inherited some of his father's bad temper. He resented criticism, was often untidy and unsuitably dressed for special occasions. He kept people waiting, seldom apologized, and was often rude and arrogant. Still he was admired and his bad behaviour accepted as the eccentric way of a genius. He was a short man – five feet four inches tall – with a small head, long black hair and, usually, a scowling face.

When Beethoven was twenty-eight the worst thing that could happen to a musician occurred: he began to go deaf and soon knew that he would lose his hearing altogether. He was depressed and lonely, but he bravely went on with his work. His career as a pianist ended, but he composed more and more marvellous music. His work became stormy and exciting and full of emotion. He began to admire courage more than anything and wrote the 'Eroica' – a heroic symphony. It was as if he could hear music with his mind. Although his last years were often lonely and unhappy he wrote some joyful music, such as

---

1821 Greek war of independence

---

the setting of the 'Ode to Joy' in his Ninth Symphony.

Beethoven died alone, but eight composers carried his coffin and the people of Vienna flocked to his grand public funeral. He had become so well known that it was only necessary to carve one word – BEETHOVEN – on his tombstone.

1822 First permanent photographs made in France

Hans Christian Andersen (1805-1875)

Hans Andersen was one of the world's greatest story-tellers. He was born in Denmark, the son of a poor shoemaker. His father died when he was only eleven and Hans had to go to work in a factory, which he hated. He was already showing a talent for poetry and at fourteen he went to Copenhagen, Denmark's capital city, hoping to find work in the theatre. He was often turned down because he was so poorly educated. He also tried to become a singer, again with no success. He was lucky enough to make a very good friend in Copenhagen, Jonas Collin, who helped him to get a royal scholarship from the king, which allowed him to go back to school and continue his education.

Soon people were talking about Hans Andersen's poetry, and he also began to write plays and novels. In 1835 he published his first fairy-story and he continued to write these tales until he died. His plays and novels are all but forgotten, except in Denmark, but his fairy-tales continue to be read by children and adults around

---

1833 Factory Act forbade work for children under nine

the world. His tales often have a message with a moral behind them. His story, 'The Ugly Duckling', about the little duckling who grew up to be a beautiful swan, is one of the most famous and well-read stories. Danny Kaye's song, 'There once was an ugly duckling . . .' makes the story impossible to forget. Some of the stories, such as 'The Emperor's New Clothes' have an adult message: the Emperor is determined to be better than everyone and dresses in the latest fashion. A tailor persuades him to have a suit made from a wonderful new material which, the tailor claims, is invisible to all but the cleverest of men. The proud Emperor will not admit that he can't see the material, wears the invisible suit and in fact goes out naked! Only an innocent, small boy is able to say 'the Emperor has no clothes on!' and make him look ridiculous.

Hans Andersen was a sensitive man who wanted to be successful and famous. He was very lonely, for although he fell in love with three women, none of them loved him and he never married. His fairy-tales, 168 of them in all, show wisdom, simplicity and humour and continue to delight. If you haven't read them you must – today!

1839 Opium war between Great Britain and China

Abraham Lincoln
(1809-1865)

Abraham Lincoln was the sixteenth president of the United States of America. He was a president who spoke out against slavery and worked hard, but unsuccessfully, to prevent a civil war. When the war came it brought victory to the North, and Lincoln worked 'with malice towards none, with charity to all' to re-establish unity between the northern and southern states of America.

Lincoln was born into a poor farming family and life was hard. The Trail, the route taken by pioneers who travelled by covered wagons to a new life in the West, passed the door of the Lincoln home. Sometimes tethered slaves went by and, at a very early age, Lincoln decided that slavery was wrong.

When he was seven the family moved to Indiana. He described it later in a letter as 'a wild region, with many bears and other wild animals still in the woods ... There were some schools, so called, but no qualification was ever required of a teacher beyond readin', writin' and cipherin'

1840 Introduction of the Penny Post in England

to the rule of three.' In the same letter he wrote: 'If any personal description of me is thought desirable, it may be said I am, in height, six feet four inches, nearly; lean in flesh, weighing on an average one hundred and eighty pounds; dark complexion, with coarse black hair and grey eyes. No other marks or brands recollected.' At the age of twenty-two, Abraham Lincoln left home and got a job as a store-keeper. He became involved in politics, and at the same time began to study law. In 1832 he stood for the Illinois State Legislature and was heavily defeated. However, he was elected in 1834, and in 1847 he went to Washington as a Republican Congressman. His political and legal careers prospered, and in 1860 he was elected President of the USA. He led the North successfully through four years of civil war, and won the support and affection of the people.

Six days after the end of the war, the President and his wife went to the theatre. The audience cheered as they entered their box. The President waved and then seemed to slump in his seat – he had been shot in the head by John Wilkes Booth, a southern fanatic. By the next morning he was dead.

His death was mourned by the nation, who had grown to respect Abraham Lincoln as a great statesman and orator. One of his best-remembered speeches was made at Gettysburg in 1863 at the dedication of a war cemetery: '. . . we here highly resolve that the dead shall not have died in vain – that this nation, under God, shall have a new birth of freedom – and that government of the people, by the people, for the people, shall not perish from the earth.'

1843 Brunel's *Great Britain* crossed the Atlantic

Charles Dickens
(1812-1870)

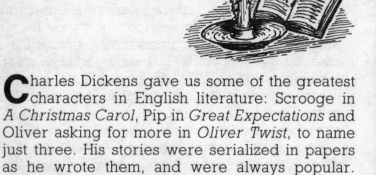

Charles Dickens gave us some of the greatest characters in English literature: Scrooge in *A Christmas Carol*, Pip in *Great Expectations* and Oliver asking for more in *Oliver Twist*, to name just three. His stories were serialized in papers as he wrote them, and were always popular. Today they are made into films and plays, and are still read by millions of people.

Charles had a good start in life in a happy family, but when he was eleven, his father lost his job and got into debt. The family had to move from their home in Chatham to a poorhouse in London, and there was not enough money for Charles to continue to go to school. Soon his father was sent to the debtors' prison at Marshalsea, and his family went with him, as was the custom at the time. Charles went to work in a factory, where blacking for cleaning shoes was made. He spent long days in a dark room, sticking labels on to jars. He hated it, but it did teach him a lot about poor people, and later helped him to put such realistic characters into his stories.

1846 Irish potato famine

Luckily, this job only lasted for a year: his father's debts were paid and Charles was able to go back to school.

Later he worked for a short time in a solicitor's office, and when he was seventeen he became a newspaper reporter and his writing career began. He worked hard, spending a lot of time reading in the British Museum, and teaching himself shorthand; he was determined to be a successful writer.

Soon the *Morning Chronicle* was paying Dickens seven guineas (£7.35) a week – a huge step up from the six shillings (30p) a week he'd earned at the factory. *Pickwick Papers* brought him quick success; people couldn't wait to read the next part of the story, and Dickens the writer had arrived.

He travelled a great deal, spending time in America, Italy and France, and giving public readings from his books. His stories are full of great characters who opened people's eyes to the hardships suffered by the poor in England. Dickens had lived in poverty and so knew what it was like to have nothing. Through his characters he was able to make the wealthy aware of the harsh life of the poor. His books are not all sadness; there is humour and happiness too; they are stories about real life as Dickens saw it.

Charles Dickens is buried in Westminster Abbey in London beside other great English writers.

1848 Marx and Engels wrote the Communist Manifesto

Queen Victoria (1819-1901)

Victoria was born at Kensington Palace in London. She became queen in 1837, when she was eighteen years old (and less than five feet tall!). Her reign lasted for sixty-four years – a period known as the Victorian Age. Her name has been given to streets, stations, a state in Australia, and to a medal, the Victoria Cross, which is the highest award that can be given for bravery.

Victoria's father died soon after she was born and she was brought up by her German mother, the Duchess of Kent. Victoria spoke only German until she was three years old. She had a lonely childhood, but was well educated by a governess and prepared for her future role. She was taught to behave correctly, and the people were delighted to have such a young queen. Victoria got on very well with Lord Melbourne, her first Prime Minister, and he became her trusted guide and friend. She didn't always get on so well with her ministers and had difficult relationships with Lord Palmerston and Gladstone.

1855 Florence Nightingale nursed in the Crimea

The young Victoria told Lord Melbourne that she was against marriage, and she wasn't keen to meet Prince Albert of Saxe-Coburg – they'd met as children and she hadn't been impressed by him. But when Albert visited Victoria at Windsor Castle in 1839, they immediately fell in love and were married in 1840. Victoria's diary tells us something of the happiness of her marriage and her four sons and five daughters.

Queen Victoria was the world's most powerful woman of her time, yet she did not support women's rights: the right to vote, to have a career, to be an MP. She believed that men should be the masters and that women were the weaker sex.

The Victorian Age was a time of invention and progress, as well as a time of contrast, when some people were incredibly rich and others desperately poor. Prince Albert planned the Great Exhibition of 1851 to celebrate the progress of the period. The Crystal Palace was built to house the exhibition; it was a huge building, made of glass, the like of which had never been seen before. Six million people visited the Crystal Palace to see its celebration of industry and life.

Victoria lived through many great, and some-times tragic, events in her long reign. She was saddened by the Crimean War, and was shocked to see how young the soldiers were. She praised Florence Nightingale, who nursed the sick and wounded soldiers in terrible conditions – there were never enough blankets or medicine to go round.

When Prince Albert died in 1861, the queen

1857 The Indian Mutiny

---

was heartbroken. She couldn't imagine life without him, and yet went on to live as a widow for another forty years. Victoria wore the black clothes of mourning and withdrew from public life. She began to lose some of her popularity – the people wanted to see their queen. Victoria tried to explain her feelings in an article in *The Times* in 1864, and did try to continue with her public duties. In 1866 the people were delighted to see their queen open Parliament, for the first time since her husband's death, and she soon regained her popularity.

Queen Victoria became Empress of India in 1874, and was given rich jewels by the Indian rajas. She developed a real interest in India. The people's love for Victoria seemed to grow as she got older. She was happy at her Golden Jubilee – all her children were married and her grandchildren delighted her. She loved the theatre and the operas of Gilbert and Sullivan. On her Diamond Jubilee, when she had been queen for sixty years, the royal procession to St Paul's Cathedral was the grandest ever seen, and was watched by cheering crowds. Later, fireworks lit up the skies of London, to end a day that no one present would ever forget. Victoria carried out her duties and was up to date with current events until a week before her death. On 22 January 1901, the Prince of Wales sent this message:

My beloved mother the Queen has just (6.30) passed away, surrounded by her children and grandchildren.
                    (signed) Albert Edward

1863 London's first underground railway

Jack the Ripper
(1800s ?)

Jack the Ripper, the only unidentified famous, or infamous, person in this book, brought terror to the streets of London's East End. Five women, all prostitutes who lived in the dark alleyways of the poorest part of London, were murdered between 31 August and 8 November 1888. Two of the victims are modelled in Madame Tussaud's Chamber of Horrors, but the murderer was never modelled, because he was never caught.

The victims were found in quiet corners with their throats cut and their bodies 'ripped' open – hence the name given to the murderer, who always vanished unseen.

The murders caused terror in the city; the chief of Scotland Yard's CID wrote in his diary, 'No one living in London that autumn will forget the terror created by these murders. Even now I can recall the foggy evenings and hear again the raucous cries of the newspaper boys, "Another horrible murder, murder, mutilation, Whitechapel!"' Even Queen Victoria commented

---

1869 The Suez Canal opened

on the terrible murders; people began to talk about the poverty and poor housing in the East End, and questions were asked in Parliament. In the eerie Chamber of Horrors, the dark, cobbled Victorian streets are reconstructed, fog whirls round the corners and the sounds of screams and running feet bring back the fears of the East-Enders in 1888.

Who was Jack the Ripper? Blood-hounds were brought from Yorkshire to help the search, but they were lost on Tooting Common. The police received letters signed 'Jack the Ripper' and there was reason to believe that he had some medical knowledge. Everybody talked about the Ripper and there were many suspects, including the queen's grandson, the Duke of Clarence. A murderer, Neill Cream, called out as he was hanged, 'I am Jack the —'. There were dozens of other suspects – even a 'Jill the Ripper', who was thought to be a midwife.

The crimes of Jack the Ripper have been remembered in films and books, but still we do not know his name.

1870 London medical school for women opened

Lord Baden-Powell
(1857-1941)

Robert Baden-Powell started the Boy Scout movement in 1908. As a boy he loved tracking animals in the woods, building camp-fires and cooking in the open air. He became a soldier when he was nineteen and enjoyed army life, both in the north-west frontiers of India and in Africa. He had a talent for tracking enemy soldiers, planning ambushes and learning to cope in the most difficult territories. He quickly became a commanding officer, and tried to pass on his skills to his soldiers. He wrote a book for them called *Aids to Scouting*.

In the war against the Boers in South Africa, he was in charge of the garrison at Mafeking, when the town was besieged for over six months. He used all his skills to hold out against the enemy and, to leave his men free for fighting, he trained young boys as messengers. He showed great courage and leadership. When Mafeking was relieved and he came home to England, he was welcomed as a hero.

Baden-Powell thought that the skills he'd taught

1870 First Education Act in England

---

his soldiers in war would be useful and fun for boys in peacetime. He took twenty-four boys to camp on Brownsea Island, off the Dorset coast. He divided them into patrols with leaders and taught them tracking, signalling, first-aid and cooking – in fact, how to be self-sufficient. There was time for fun as well and the day usually ended with story-telling and a sing-song around a camp-fire. From this camp, and his book, *Scouting for Boys*, the Boy Scout movement grew.

Soon there were Scout Troops around the country and by the time of Lord Baden-Powell's death, the movement was flourishing in one hundred countries. Cubs, Rangers, Girl Guides and Brownies followed and, although the movement has changed a great deal over the years, it still continues to attract millions of young people today.

In 1920 Lord Baden-Powell was made Chief Scout of the World. In 1938 he returned to the Africa he had always loved, and died in Kenya in 1941.

1876 Alexander Bell invented the telephone

Mahatma Gandhi
(1869-1948)

Millions of Indians still talk of Gandhi as Bapu, father of the nation, and his face is well known to people all round the world. He was born Mohandas Gandhi, at a time when India had been ruled by Britain for nearly 300 years. Some states were ruled by princes loyal to the British, and Gandhi's father was the Diwan, the Prime Minister, of Porbandar, a small state on the west coast. The family were Hindus and spoke Gujarati; they hoped that Mohandas would one day take his father's place as Diwan. With this in mind, he was sent to England for three years to study law. He returned to work in a legal practice in Bombay, but soon decided to take a job in South Africa. He was there for twenty-one years and helped Indians to fight against South Africa's unjust laws.

South Africa was a shock to Gandhi and his experience there changed his life. On his arrival, he was forced out of a first-class train compartment because he was not white. He soon realized that the Indians in South Africa suffered daily

---

1889 Eiffel Tower built in Paris

---

insults and were treated almost like slaves. Gandhi quickly lost his early shyness and began to speak out at public meetings. He was convinced that change would only be brought about by non-violent means. After much campaigning and many periods in prison, General Smuts, the South African leader, gave way on the main issues and Gandhi decided it was time to return to India.

The Gandhi returning home was much changed. He started a community based on the ideas of service to others and non-violence, and began to work to break down the Hindu caste system. The lowest caste, the Untouchables, were not allowed into temples and Gandhi shocked many people by bringing an untouchable family into his community, or ashram.

Like his family, Gandhi had been loyal to the British. This changed when, in 1919, General Dyer ordered his soldiers to fire on the crowd outside the Sikh Golden Temple in Amritsar. Nearly 400 men, women and children were killed and thousands more were wounded. In 1920 Gandhi became President of the All-India Home Rule League and, later, leader of the Indian National Congress, working for India's independence. He called for civil disobedience and non-co-operation with the British. There were outbreaks of violence and Gandhi blamed and punished himself by fasting. He was sent to prison, but continued his work as soon as he was released – he was one of the first leaders to talk of equality for women.

In 1930 Gandhi led a 200-mile march to the sea

1894 Rudyard Kipling wrote the first *Jungle Book*

to collect salt – salt was taxed and only the Government could take it from the sea – soon illegal salt was available all over India. Thousands, including Gandhi, were imprisoned. In 1931 he was released and went to London to attend a conference about India's future. He refused to stay in a hotel and chose instead an East End hostel for poor people. He went to tea at Buckingham Palace dressed as usual in his dhoti. He said, 'The king was wearing enough for both of us!' On return to India, he was soon back in prison, fasting again and prepared to fast to death if this was necessary.

In the 1940s work continued to get the British to leave India. Gandhi had always worried about the troubles and violence between Hindus and Muslims, and he walked from village to village trying to persuade people to end this violence and live peacefully.

In 1947 India became independent and, from a part of India, a new country, Pakistan, a Muslim country, was born. To Gandhi the granting of independence was 'the noblest act of the British nation'. He was horrified at the outbreak of violence between Muslims and Hindus in which many thousands died. Again he fasted for peace. Before the new India had settled down, Mahatma Gandhi was murdered, shot at a prayer meeting. To many, Gandhi was a saint; the world was shocked by his death and today he is remembered for his work as a peace-maker.

1900 Founding of the British Labour Party

Vladimir Ilyich Lenin
(1870-1924)

Vladimir Ilyich Ulanov grew up in a quiet Russian town. He changed his name to Lenin, which was to become one of the most well-known names of the twentieth century. His father, a school inspector, worked hard to educate his six children. The family lived happily in a comfortable wooden house until, when Vladimir was fifteen, his father died. The Ulanovs were luckier than most Russians: the country's huge population included about eighty million peasants who didn't get enough to eat when the harvests were bad. A small number of very rich families lived in beautiful houses in Moscow or St Petersburg, and owned large estates in the country. The richest person of all was the Emperor of Russia, the Czar, who was all-powerful and ruled the country as he wished.

The educated people began to speak out against the huge gap between rich and poor. Vladimir's elder brother, Saçha, joined a group of students who tried to murder Czar Alexander III. He was caught and was hanged in 1887 – his death had a great effect on his brother.

1903 Emily Pankhurst fought for votes for women

Vladimir was a good scholar. He studied law at Kazan University and he loved to read, argue and discuss. When he was eighteen he read *Das Kapital* by Karl Marx – it described a revolution of the working classes and a move towards socialism, when all property would belong to the people. After Sacha's death, Vladimir's mother tried to keep Vladimir away from politics, but this was impossible.

Millions of people starved after the famine in 1891, and Vladimir decided to move to St Petersburg, the capital city. He worked in a law office, spending his spare time talking to working people about revolution and about their lives of hardship. In 1895, after an illness, Vladimir's mother sent him abroad to improve his health. He met other Marxists and his belief in the ideas of Marx strengthened. When he returned home he was searched at the border and from then on he was always watched by the police.

In December 1895 Vladimir and his revolutionary friends were arrested and sent to prison, and then to exile in Siberia. Lenin spent his time reading, writing and planning his revolution. In 1900 he was freed, but was forbidden to live in St Petersburg; he continued with his underground activities. He published a secret revolutionary newspaper called *Iskra*, which means the Spark. He continued to publish when, once again, he was forced to live in exile – this time in London, where he continued to develop his ideas.

Meanwhile in Russia thousands of people marched on the Winter Palace to ask Czar Nicholas II for better conditions for workers – police

1906 San Francisco earthquake

and soldiers fired on the crowd and many were killed. Lenin was unhappy about the way things were going and continued with his own plans.

The Great War broke out in 1914 and brought more hardship to the Russian people. In February 1917 revolution came again, and this time the soldiers refused to obey the Czar's orders to open fire. The Czar was forced to give up his throne and a provisional government was set up. Lenin returned home to a hero's welcome. He spoke of his plans and changed the name of his party to the Communist Party. Unrest continued and another revolt broke out at Trotsky's headquarters in the Smolny Convent. Lenin went in disguise to join Trotsky. The end of the provisional government was announced and the Congress of Soviets, led by Lenin, came into power. Lenin called for an end to war, and an end to the private ownership of land. He was appointed President and so became the leader of Russia – an almost impossible job, the ruling of Russia, had to be tackled.

Russia was a hard land to govern. Lenin struggled for three years to end rebellions; he dealt violently with those who worked against him. In 1922 he introduced his new economic policy and criticism of the party was forbidden. Lenin tried to keep his vision, but his health was failing and Communist leaders were becoming a new ruling class, battling over the future.

Lenin died in 1924. His coffin was carried to Moscow – the twenty-mile route was lined with weeping people – the father of their revolution was dead. His body was embalmed in a crystal casket in a mausoleum in Red Square. He was remembered almost as a god, pictures of him were displayed everywhere, his words were quoted and thousands filed past his body every day. He was revered until about 1988, when Mikhail Gorbachev's policies of 'perestroika' and 'glasnost' allowed the people to look again at their country's past.

Sir Winston Churchill
(1874-1965)

Winston Churchill became a member of the House of Commons in 1900, when Queen Victoria was on the throne, and left the House in 1963 during the reign of Queen Elizabeth II. He was one of the longest-serving members of Parliament.

Winston was a lonely child, his parents had little time for him and seemed to offer him no parental love. His nanny was important to him in his early life, even after he was sent away to boarding-school at the age of seven. He didn't do well at school and experienced his first success at Sandhurst, where he trained for the army. He enjoyed his years as a soldier and at the same time he began to develop as a writer, particularly as a newspaper reporter. The young Churchill fought in Cuba (where he got his taste for cigars), India, Egypt and South Africa. After the Boer War he returned to England as a hero and, in 1900, he began his parliamentary career.

Winston Churchill's career was always lively and hitting the headlines, especially when he

1917 Clarence Birdseye started freezing food

moved from the Conservative Party to the Liberal Party and back again. He was a man who had to follow his own convictions, even if that meant going against the party line and becoming unpopular. Alongside his political career, he found time to paint and to write many books on history and biography.

His time of greatness came when, in 1940, the power of Germany was growing, and England was threatened by the advancing German armies. Neville Chamberlain resigned as Prime Minister and King George VI invited Churchill to replace him. Churchill would speak to the people in slow, gruff tones that few could resist. On taking office he made his famous speech, 'I have nothing to offer but blood, toil, tears and sweat . . . You ask what is our aim? It is victory! Victory at all costs. Victory in spite of all terror. Victory, however long and hard the road may be.'

During the war, Churchill often worked a twenty-hour day. He soon became a familiar figure wearing his siren suit, smoking a big cigar and giving his famous victory sign with the first two fingers of his hand.

There are mixed opinions of Sir Winston Churchill's career, but it is clear that he had the qualities that were necessary to lead a country through war-time. He led Great Britain and her allies to victory in World War II and it is for this that he is most remembered.

Pablo Picasso
(1881-1973)

Pablo Picasso entered the world in dramatic style in 1881. The midwife who delivered him thought he was dead and left him on a table while she looked after his mother. Luckily an uncle rushed for a doctor and saved him from suffocation.

Picasso's father was an art teacher and professor of fine art, and taught his son a lot about painting and art in general. The young boy started to use a pencil before he could speak and sat for hours drawing spirals; later he loved being on the beach and drawing pictures in the sand, and by 1897 his pictures were being exhibited.

Picasso studied in Barcelona and Madrid, and then moved to Paris in 1904. For the rest of his life he made his home in France, but he never became a French citizen and instead remained a proud Spaniard at heart. Picasso's influence on the art of the twentieth century is legendary; his output was enormous and his art moved through distinct stages in his long, and often tempestuous, life.

1922 Howard Carter opened Tutankhamun's tomb

One of his most famous pictures, painted in 1937, is called *Guernica* and is Picasso's personal outcry against the Spanish Civil War. Like most Spanish children, Picasso had been taken to bull-fights and in *Guernica* he used the symbols of the fight – the bull, representing evil, towering above the dying horse, representing good, and symbolizing the terrible suffering of the Spanish people. After the victory of General Franco and the Fascists in the civil war, Picasso became an exile – he wouldn't return to a Spain ruled by Franco, and he would not allow *Guernica* to go to Spain either. The picture was kept on display in New York for many years and was only returned to Spain after the death of Franco in 1975. Pablo Picasso never returned to Spain.

In 1944 Picasso joined the French Communist Party and designed his famous *Peace Poster* for the 1949 Paris Peace Congress. Since then his white dove has become accepted throughout the world as a symbol of peace. In 1912 some of Picasso's Cubist drawings and paintings were shown in London – they were sold for between two and twenty pounds each. Today when his pictures are up for sale they cost millions of pounds!

1925 One million people unemployed in England

Adolf Hitler
(1889-1945)

A wax model of Adolf Hitler stands at the entrance to Madame Tussaud's Chamber of Horrors. How did Hitler, an ordinary boy, a dull pupil at school who began work as a house-painter, become so infamous? He was born in Austria and went to Vienna when he was nineteen – he wanted to be an artist, but the Vienna Art Academy wouldn't have him. He tried to make a living by painting and selling his own postcards. This was not a success, so he was very poor and lived like a tramp. The young Adolf spent a lot of time arguing with other down-and-outs about politics – his were already the politics of hate as he blamed all that was wrong on the Jews or the Communists.

In 1913 Hitler moved to Germany and when World War I started he joined the army. He seemed to enjoy the war and he won a medal, the Iron Cross, for bravery.

After the war there was great hardship for many German people – unemployment and food shortages were growing. Hitler and his friends

---

1926 General Strike in England

---

started the National Socialist Party, which quickly became known as the Nazi Party, and talk of revolution began. In 1923 he was sent to prison when a Nazi attempt to bring down the Bavarian Government failed. In prison he wrote *Mein Kampf* (My Struggle), expressing his ideas; these were soon taken up by the growing Nazi Party. In a time of unemployment and growing poverty people look for change, and the German people responded to Hitler's promise of power for the working class. Growing numbers joined the party and even the children flocked to join the Hitler Youth movement.

In 1933 Adolf Hitler became Chancellor of Germany and his policies of hate and mastery, and his greed for territory, led to the outbreak of World War II, to concentration camps and persecution, to millions of deaths, and finally to the defeat of Germany.

Hitler is often called a megalomaniac – someone with an insane passion for power. He survived an attempt to kill him, but in the final years of the war his health worsened and he virtually lived on drugs. On 30 April 1945, when the Russian soldiers were close to his Berlin headquarters, Adolf Hitler and his wife of one day, Eva Braun, committed suicide together. Somehow that dull schoolboy had developed the authority to persuade a nation to follow a policy of hate and mass murder – his career was a wholly evil one.

1928 Walt Disney created Mickey Mouse

Charles de Gaulle
(1890-1970)

Charles de Gaulle's life was ruled by a passion to serve France. His family were intellectuals with strong religious and political ideas, and Charles grew up with a love of history, and a dream of becoming a great soldier. He had extraordinary self-confidence and always stood out from the crowd. He was enormously tall and could easily dominate any gathering.

De Gaulle became a soldier. He fought bravely in World War I and soon became a brilliant staff officer. When World War II started he was a colonel fighting the highly efficient German army with an ill-equipped, ill-prepared division of soldiers. In 1940 de Gaulle became Under Secretary of State for War. Eleven days later, the French army collapsed and the Government retreated from Paris. As France fell to the Germans, General de Gaulle fled to England to raise the standard of the Free French Army. At the time of the liberation of France in 1944, he led one of the first forces to enter Paris. He was welcomed home and was met everywhere by huge, enthusiastic crowds.

1929 Collapse of New York stock exchange

The politics of peace didn't seem to suit de Gaulle, and in 1946 he retired from politics because of the lack of unity between the parties. He lived in retirement and was rarely seen in public until 1958. This time France was in trouble with Algeria and again it fell to de Gaulle to act when, in May 1958, he was asked to be President of France. He led France through the difficult years of conflict with Algeria; he wasn't always agreed with, but he seemed to be the only person who could win the confidence and support of the French people.

In 1970 de Gaulle resigned as President. He had steered France through another period of turmoil, had granted independence to all France's colonies in Africa, had blocked Britain's entry to the European Economic Community, had argued with world leaders and he had shown extraordinary courage in his own convictions.

Charles de Gaulle has a place in history because he responded to the needs of his country. He was able to lead the people from defeat in 1940, and through conflict in the 1960s. He never represented a political party, he simply represented France, and for this the people followed him.

1931 Frankenstein made Boris Karloff a star

Agatha Christie
(1890-1976)

gatha Christie is famous as a writer of crime and detective novels. From the time her first book was published in 1920, she produced at least a book a year – a new 'Christie for Christmas' came to be expected by her readers. That first book, *The Mysterious Affair at Styles*, was turned down by four publishers before it was finally accepted – at the time it made twenty-five pounds for Agatha Christie.

Agatha grew up in Devon and her first writing success came when she was eleven, when a poem she had written on a visit to her grandmother in Ealing was printed in the local paper. In her twenties she nursed soldiers who had been injured in World War I and she also worked in the hospital dispensary. It was then that she learned about poisons – knowledge that would be very useful in her career as a crime writer. The young Agatha loved reading the stories of Sherlock Holmes, and soon started work on her own detective story. Her famous detective, Hercule Poirot, appeared in her first book. He was not a very

---

1934 Mao led 'The Long March' in China

romantic figure, and was described thus by Agatha on his first appearance: 'He was hardly more than five feet, four inches, but carried himself with great dignity. His head was exactly the shape of an egg, and he always perched it a little to one side. His moustache was very stiff and military. The neatness of his attire was almost incredible; I believe a speck of dust would have caused him more pain than a bullet wound.' Hercule Poirot and Miss Jane Marple, an inquisitive village lady who solved many a mystery, are Agatha Christie's most-loved characters. They never met because, in spite of many readers' requests, they never appeared in the same book. By 1962 Agatha Christie was said to be the most widely read British author – Shakespeare came a poor second!

Agatha Christie also wrote plays – the most well-known, *The Mousetrap*, opened in London in 1952 and is still running. On its opening, Agatha gave all rights in it to her nine-year-old grandson; by 1982 the play had made him a millionaire. *The Mousetrap* was once performed in Wormwood Scrubs prison, and two prisoners managed to escape while everyone else was gripped by the mystery!

One incident in Agatha Christie's life was as strange as her stories. In 1926, after a quarrel with her first husband, Agatha mysteriously disappeared. Her abandoned car was found near a lake at a popular beauty spot – the lights were still on and her clothes and driving-licence were inside. The newspapers made the most of the story, rewards were offered and thousands of

---

1936 Civil war in Spain

---

people joined in the search for Agatha. There were theories of suicide, murder and loss of memory and, although she was found safe and sound a week later, in a Harrogate hotel, registered in another name, the mystery of her disappearance has never really been solved.

1937 Tolkien wrote *The Hobbit*

John Fitzgerald Kennedy (1917-1963)

John Fitzgerald Kennedy was the thirty-fifth president of the United States of America. He was elected in 1960 by the smallest majority ever. He was the youngest of America's presidents and the first Roman Catholic one. In his short time at the White House, the official home of America's president, his family became almost like a royal family. He and his wife Jacqueline were always in the news, and she became a leader of fashion. Events in their children's lives were widely reported and the evening 'children's hour' in the White House was copied by many American families. The White House had been a formal, rather old-fashioned place until the Kennedy family made it into a home. Jacqueline redecorated it and gave the American people a televised tour of the house.

John Kennedy was born into a rich family and his father had always wanted one of his sons to enter politics and stand for the presidency. When Joe, his eldest son, was killed, John was expected to enter politics. He was in the navy during World

1939 World War II began

War II and won medals for bravery and leadership. When the war was over John worked briefly as a newspaper reporter and then entered politics and, at the age of twenty-nine, he became a Congress member for Massachusetts. In 1960 the Democratic Party nominated him as their candidate for the presidency and he fought against the Republican, Richard Nixon. The candidates were seen together in the first-ever televised debate and the people began to recognize Kennedy, who looked good and performed well in the debates. He won the election and was sworn in as President in January 1961.

In 1962 Kennedy stood up to Khrushchev, the leader of the Soviet Union, who was building up missile strength in Cuba, within easy reach of the USA. Kennedy ordered a blockade of Cuba until the Russian bases and missiles were removed. It was a time of fear – would there be war? The world held its breath. Within a month Khrushchev backed down, the bases were closed and the Soviet troops went home. John Kennedy's reputation was made.

Kennedy wasn't always popular – he made enemies in the South when he pushed for a Civil Rights bill to give equal rights to America's black people – but he was always in the news. There had been many threats on his life – 860 during his first year as President – and there were more when his plan to visit Dallas, Texas, on 22 November 1963 was announced. What happened has become part of history: the three shots, the screams, the picture of Jacqueline cradling her husband's head in her lap, blood staining her

---

1944 Secondary education for all in England

dress, the rush to hospital and then the announce-ment that President Kennedy was dead. America was in a state of shock.

Kennedy's funeral was attended by leaders from all over the world and a flame still burns on his grave.

1945 Atom bombs dropped on Hiroshima and Nagasaki

Nelson Mandela
(1918-)

Nelson Mandela is the son of an African chief. His Xhosa name is Rolihlahla, but, as was the custom, he was also given a heroic European name – Nelson, after the famous English admiral. As a boy Nelson helped on the land, learnt to hunt and listened to stories told about the days before the white men came. As he grew up he was shocked to find that his proud background was looked down on by the white government of South Africa.

When he was twenty-two, Nelson Mandela went to Johannesburg where he saw that life was very different for black and white people. Like all black people, he had to obey the hated Pass Laws – a pass was needed to get a job, to live in a town, to travel and even to be out after eleven o'clock at night.

Mandela met Walter Sisulu who became his friend, helped him to study law and awakened his interest in the African National Congress (ANC). The ANC had been started in 1912, aiming to unite the African people against the

---

1948 Olympic Games in London

unfair laws of the white government. In 1948 the Government began to push for apartheid, a system separating the races of the country. Mandela became an active member of the ANC, fighting for black dignity and against unjust laws. It was clear that he was an exceptional leader as he moved around the country speaking to huge crowds of people. He soon attracted the attention of the authorities and, in 1952, he went to prison for the first time – for being out after eleven p.m. without a pass! Bans on his activities increased and the more active Mandela tried to be in the fight against apartheid, the more difficult the authorities made his life.

In 1960 in the small town of Sharpeville, the police fired on a crowd protesting against the Pass Laws – sixty-nine Africans were killed and many more wounded, most were shot in the back. Anger and horror led to riots and demonstrations. The Government declared a state of emergency and banned the ANC, making it an illegal organization. Nelson Mandela lived rather like an outlaw, fighting for the freedom of his people, until he was arrested in 1962. By now he was so well known that in the townships people painted the slogan, FREE MANDELA, on their walls. He was accused of encouraging African workers to strike and of leaving the country without the correct papers. For this he was sentenced to five years in prison.

A year later he was on trial again, accused with eight others of planning guerrilla war and encouraging rebellion. Nelson Mandela spoke to the court for over four hours about the ANC's fight

---

1948 Birth of the state of Israel

against racism, and determination to have equal political rights, to have the vote on the same terms as white people. Mandela said it was a fight he was willing to die for. Eight of the accused, including Mandela, were found guilty and sentenced to life imprisonment. The seven black men sentenced were sent to Robben Island maximum security prison; the eighth man, a white man, was taken to join white political prisoners in Pretoria. Robben Island is a small, rocky island about six miles from Cape Town; it is a place of hardship, suffering and loneliness. Nelson Mandela was to remain in prison for twenty-six years.

During his imprisonment, Mandela was never forgotten: his wife Winnie, his people, and ANC members in South Africa and abroad, kept up the pressure on the Government to free him. He became almost more important in prison than he was when free; he came to symbolize the fight for freedom for the black people of South Africa. After twenty-six years, and in his seventies, Nelson Mandela proudly walked free again. The twenty-six years had not defeated him and he was ready to take up the fight again.

Today he talks to the leaders of the world as well as to his own people, today there are signs of change in South Africa, and today Nelson Mandela continues to lead his people in their fight for freedom and equality.

Marilyn Monroe
(1926-1962)

When Marilyn Monroe started to work in films in 1946, she was just one of many starlets taken on for her good looks and instant sex appeal. But she is the one who is remembered; her face still appears frequently and she is recognized world-wide. Is it because of the mystery surrounding her death?

She grew up as Norma Jean Baker, an unwanted child who lived in many temporary foster homes, where her mother used to visit her. When Norma Jean was only seven, her mother was admitted to a mental hospital, and Norma Jean was left even more alone. She spent time in a Los Angeles orphanage and went to High School, but dropped out when she was just sixteen to marry for the first time.

She worked as a model until she was given a screen test, which led to a film contract and to her changing her name to Marilyn Monroe. She played the dumb-blonde role in several films and was promoted by her studio as their 'blonde bombshell'. Soon she was famous. Her marriages,

---

1952 Pocket transistor radios on sale

---

to an American baseball player and to the intellectual playwright, Arthur Miller, increased people's interest in her life and she was always in the news. Marilyn took acting lessons and desperately wanted to be seen as a serious actress rather than as a sex object. She did prove in *Some Like It Hot* that she had real ability as a comedy actress.

Her life was short and often unhappy, and she suffered increasingly from mental and emotional stress. Her relationships were difficult and often short-lived, and she was sacked from her final film contract because she kept failing to turn up for shoots. In August 1962 she was found dead in her Los Angeles home after taking an overdose of sleeping pills. She had moved from being a homeless waif to a symbol of her time, a woman who the world found fascinating. More books have been written about Marilyn Monroe than about any other film actress. Still stories are being told about her life, her loves and friendships with the famous – her name has even been linked with that of President Kennedy. Still a sense of mystery surrounds both her life and her death.

1953 Hillary and Tenzing climbed Mount Everest

Margaret Thatcher
(1926-)

In 1979 Margaret Thatcher became Britain's first ever woman prime minister. After the Conservative victory in the general election, she was called to Buckingham Palace and the Queen asked her to form a government. Like the wives of previous prime ministers, Denis Thatcher waited downstairs at the Palace while his wife, Margaret Thatcher, had an audience with Queen Elizabeth II. For the first time in history, the two most important positions in the land were held by women.

Margaret Hilda Roberts was the daughter of a Grantham grocer – her parents ran the grocery shop and the family lived in a flat above it. Margaret was always serious-minded, with a determination to win – whether it was a poetry-reading competition, a hockey match or a place at Oxford University. She studied Chemistry at Oxford, but was already interested in politics. She joined the Oxford University Conservative Association and became its chairman. She couldn't join in the famous Oxford Union debates because women

---

1957 European Economic Community set up

members were still not accepted!

After her graduation, Margaret worked as a research chemist and, when she was only twenty-three, she stood as a Conservative candidate in the general election. Dartford was a safe Labour area and she was not elected. She went on to study law and worked as a barrister until she was elected to the House of Commons in 1959, as the Conservative member for Finchley. She soon became a junior minister and, in 1970, she joined Edward Heath's Cabinet as Minister for Education and Science. She was not always popular and when she introduced a bill stopping free milk for older school children she became known as 'Margaret Thatcher, milk-snatcher'.

In 1975 Mrs Thatcher stood against Edward Heath in the party's leadership election and won. She led the Tories in opposition and, when the party won the 1979 election, she became Prime Minister. Her government promised to reduce the power of the unions, to cut taxes and to give economic freedom – this freedom meant cutting back on welfare spending and privatizing public-sector industries. Margaret Thatcher wanted to change society; to return to the Victorian values of hard work, self-reliance, duty and respect for the family. The economy was slow to move and some believe that it was only the British victory in the Falklands War in 1982 that won the next election for Mrs Thatcher.

Early in her leadership Margaret Thatcher was nicknamed 'The Iron Lady', because her determination was always strong and clear. She showed extraordinary energy, worked long hours, and entered every House of Commons question-time confident that she'd done her homework and could respond to whatever the opposition threw at her. She survived many serious attacks on her government and seemed unbeatable, even though her economic policies, and her health and education changes were often unpopular. She was said to rule her Cabinet like a dictator and to control the party rather than to work co-operatively. Half-way through her third term as Prime Minister she talked of going 'on and on', and for a long time it was difficult to see who could stop her.

Towards the end of 1990, opinion polls showed Labour's growing popularity. Behind the scenes things were not well in the Conservative Party. When Mrs Thatcher stood alone against the members of the European Community and stridently declared that she was right, her party turned against her. She was challenged for the leadership and in December 1990, she resigned, leaving the party in the hands of John Major. It all happened so quickly that it was hard to realize she had gone.

1961 Yuri Gagarin became the first man in space

Queen Elizabeth II and her family
(1926-)

Britain's monarchy is one of the oldest in the world and has changed its role over the years. Gone are the days when a queen could say, 'off with his head', and know that the order would be carried out. Instead the Queen today is a figure-head, a symbol, but she and her family are still popular with the British people and, as one of the few remaining ruling royal families, they are fascinating to people all over the world.

Elizabeth became Queen in 1952 when she was only twenty-five, the wife of a Naval Lieutenant, Philip Mountbatten, and the mother of a three-year-old son, Charles, and a one-year-old daughter, Anne. The monarchy has become more public during Elizabeth's reign and seldom does a day pass without the papers finding something to report about the Queen or her family; the royal faces have become some of the most widely recognized faces in the world. The royals are now called by their first names and people talk about them as though they really know them. Since Elizabeth's grandfather, George V, made

---

1963 The Beatles are all the craze

the first Christmas broadcast to his people in 1932, this custom has grown and now the Queen is seen on television on Christmas Day, with members of her family, and this brings her into the homes of many of her people.

There's still, of course, pomp and ceremony, as the Queen is the Head of State. Ceremonies such as the Opening of Parliament and the Trooping the Colour, continue, but not without change. The Queen for many years rode her horse side-saddle to inspect her troops on Horse Guards' Parade, now, though still dressed in full uniform, she walks. Royal tours continue but with walkabouts among the crowds instead of the old formality.

The Queen's children also find it hard to have a private life. Prince Charles was welcomed into the world in November 1948 by the ringing of bells of St Paul's Cathedral and Westminster Abbey, and by cheering crowds outside Buckingham Palace, where he was born. When he was a baby his nanny took him out to St James's Park in his pram and there were no fears for his safety. By the time he was three, public interest had grown and walks were in more private places and were always in the company of a nearby detective. Security and interest have continued and when, as Prince of Wales, he married Lady Diana Spencer in 1981, the whole nation watched. Charles, as the future king, appears often in public – his upbringing has been unlike that of previous kings, and he will be the first king to have been educated at school. In the past, royal princes and princesses were educated by tutors

---

1965 American offensive in Vietnam

---

or governesses at home, and were never given the chance to mix with children of their own age as equals. Already, Prince William, Charles and Diana's first son, is at school and everything he does, both good and bad, is reported in all the newspapers.

Queen Elizabeth II's name will go down in history; she has become more well known than any previous monarch. Her family too – her husband Philip, her mother Elizabeth, her sister Margaret, her four children Charles, Anne, Andrew and Edward, and her daughters-in-law, Diana and Sarah, are all public figures.

1967 First heart transplant operation

Martin Luther King
(1929-1968)

In 1964 Martin Luther King was given the Nobel Peace Prize. He deserved this prize as much as any of the winners, for although he was often threatened by violence, he always replied with talk of peace and Christian love. His strength and courage gave dignity, as well as justice, to his cause – full civil rights for the black people of America. Rights that white people took for granted. Abraham Lincoln had freed the slaves; Martin Luther King gave their descendants self-respect and the beginnings of real freedom.

In 1955 Rosa Parks, a black American, got on a bus in Montgomery, Alabama. She had been shopping and was tired and very pleased to get a seat on the bus. Some white men got on and it was expected at that time that any black person would give their seat to a white person. Rosa refused to give up her seat and was taken to court by the bus company and fined. The black people of Montgomery were angry and refused to use the buses until polite and fair treatment was promised. A group of them joined together to fight for

---

1968 Soviet invasion of Czechoslovakia

equal rights, and Martin Luther King, a young Baptist minister, became their leader. Many white Americans were furious to think that black people dared to argue with them. Martin Luther King and his followers were threatened and abused. Many wanted to respond violently, but their leader would not allow this. Soon their campaign was noticed and in Washington the Supreme Court granted black people the same rights as white people on the country's buses. This first success led to a growing movement for equality, for the right to vote, the right to the same educational and career opportunities as white people, for the right to travel on any bus and to eat in any restaurant. Martin Luther King's courage was endless: he didn't let threats and violence stop him. He was not afraid of death and believed, 'Every man should have something he'd die for. A man who won't die for something isn't fit to live.'

In 1963 the now famous civil rights march took place in Washington, with tens of thousands of people, black and white, marching to the Abraham Lincoln memorial. Martin Luther King, in ringing tones full of emotion, made his memorable speech, 'I have a dream that one day this nation will rise up, live out the true meaning of its creed . . . that all men are created equal. This will be the day when all God's children will be able to sing with new meaning "Let Freedom ring".'

Other black leaders wanted to fight those who threatened their cause, but Martin Luther King preached non-violence to the end. He knew his enemies would get him, the threats continued,

---

1969 Neil Armstrong walked on the moon

his house was bombed and, in 1968, when he was only thirty-eight, he was shot dead by a white man. He had started his people along the road to freedom, but there was still a long way to go.

Mikhail Gorbachev
(1931-)

Mikhail Gorbachev's name is widely known throughout the world, as are his face, his voice, his beliefs and his wife! This is unusual for a leader of the Soviet Union, but goes with his most famous policy, 'glasnost', which means openness. Until 1985 when Gorbachev became General Secretary of the Communist Party of the Soviet Union, and so head of the Government, policies were based on secrecy rather than on openness. After the Csar's defeat in the 1917 Revolution, the Communists came to power and based their rule on the thoughts of Marx and Lenin. The October Revolution was meant to end the absolute rule of the Csars and to build a society based on equality; a society in which everything would be owned communally. Lenin was the first leader of the Communist Party and laws were soon passed to give new benefits, including free education, to all the people. Lenin soon realized that it was not easy to change society, food was in short supply, the country was involved in wars and there was great suffering.

1973 Britain joined the EEC

People disappeared to concentration camps and Stalin, who followed Lenin as leader, was more cruel than any Csar and was responsible for the deaths of millions of people. For seventy years, discussion of the troubles of the Soviet Union was not allowed, Lenin's picture was everywhere and he was almost worshipped. The press was controlled by the Government, and writers and scientists were censored and imprisoned if they tried to speak out.

The USSR grew in strength and became, along with the USA, one of the world's superpowers. The space programme was impressive, the arms build-up was frightening and Soviet rule spread to much of Eastern Europe. The outsiders' view was of an indestructible system, but the people's lives were hard and progress was slow.

Almost seventy years after the revolution, Mikhail Gorbachev came to power, a different leader wanting to introduce 'perestroika', a re-structuring of society, and a spirit of 'glasnost' or openness. For the first time the crimes of Stalin could be openly discussed and written about and the past was available to the Soviet people.

Mikhail Gorbachev was born into a peasant family and missed his first term at school because he didn't have the right clothes and shoes to wear. Later he studied law at Moscow University. He also took a course in Communist Philosophy and soon realized that the ideas were not like the reality he saw around him. As was normal, he joined the Communist Party and his personality and intelligence helped him to progress to senior

---

1980 War between Iraq and Iran

positions, and eventually to become General Secretary in 1985.

Gorbachev's leadership is almost western – he talks to the people, appears on television and travels in the USSR and abroad with his wife Raisa. Now, millions of non-Soviets know two Russian words – perestroika and glasnost – and these policies offered hope to the Soviet people who look to Gorbachev to lead them into the future. Now, the first dream is over, Gorbachev, like Lenin before him, has found out how hard it is to change society. The USSR is going through a time of uncertainty; many republics are trying to break away and become independent; the economy is collapsing and people are becoming impatient because the promised change is so slow to happen. Boris Yeltsin, the leader of the Russian Republic, is challenging Gorbachev's leadership. The future is unknown but what is certain is that Mikhail Gorbachev has changed the course of the Soviet Union, and there can be no going back. Can Gorbachev see his country through to democracy? Only time will tell.

1982 Britain and Argentina at war over the Falklands

Elvis Presley
(1935-1977)

Elvis Presley is remembered as the most adulated performer of the rock 'n' roll era. With his good looks and amazing sex appeal, he had his fans screaming and fainting at his feet. His music mixed the black and white styles, and was revolutionary; his voice was like no other and his almost secret, slightly sideways smile seemed to be aimed at every individual in his audience and to quickly have them under his spell.

Elvis was born into poverty, and his twin brother Jesse died at birth. Life was a struggle and Elvis grew up having a very strong relationship with his mother. The gospel music of his early years influenced him and, once he got started in the music business, he hurtled to fame and success. His fame brought him almost too much publicity; he was mobbed by his fans and was forced into becoming almost a prisoner in his home – Gracelands – a house of unbelievable wealth and excess.

After his first big hits, 'Heartbreak Hotel' and 'Blue Suede Shoes', his life was never the same

---

1986 Nuclear accident at Chernobyl

again. There were wild scenes at his concerts as fans responded to his gyrating performances and his extraordinary sexuality. His career was interrupted for two years when he was drafted to Germany, as a soldier in the United States army, but his popularity was not affected. Even his marriage to Priscilla in 1967 did not deter the adoration of his fans.

Elvis made many films but most of them, such as *Love Me Tender* and *Jailhouse Rock*, were just vehicles for his songs. His music and his films deteriorated towards the end of his life, but his fans still remained loyal.

By the mid-seventies Elvis increasingly withdrew to his Gracelands estate in Memphis with his family and his bodyguards. He became dependent on drugs and gained lots of weight. His death at the age of forty-two was found to be from 'natural causes', but the sensationalist press never accepted this. There were hysterical crowds outside Gracelands when the news of his death was given, and Presley products went on to break all sales records. Books and documentaries still seek to examine his life, and to investigate the cause of his withdrawal to Gracelands and his early death.

Elvis Presley holds every rock record in the United Kingdom including most Top Ten hits and most weeks in the charts – he is a legend.

1990 The Berlin Wall came down

Index

THE PUFFIN BOOK OF HANDWRITING
Tom Gourdie

How to write well with everyday materials. Write an alphabet in a tree of hearts, fill in word puzzles, trace letters, draw line patterns, have fun and acquire an elegant style of hand-writing. These exercises have been devised to help you learn how to write beautifully.

PETS FOR KEEPS
Dick King-Smith

Keeping a pet can be fascinating and great fun. You don't have to be an expert either. But it is important to choose the right pet: one that will fit in with your family and surround-ings, one that you can afford to keep, one that you will enjoy looking after, and – most important – one that will be happy with you. This book is packed with useful information about budgies, hamsters, cats, guinea-pigs, mice, rabbits, gerbils, canaries, bantams, rats, goldfish and dogs.

CHECK OUT CHESS
Bob Wade and Ted Nottingham

A basic guide for those learning to play chess. The moves each piece can make are described and there are a variety of exercises to familiarise the reader with them. The principles of checking, castling and so on are clearly explained, as are attacking, defending and the rudiments of tactics.

EUROPE: UP AND AWAY
Sue Finnie

A lively book packed with information about Western Europe which includes sections on stamps, car numbers and languages as well as topics related to an individual country (from Flamenco dancing to frogs' legs).

WATCH OUT: Keeping safe outdoors
Rosie Leyden and Suzanne Ahwai

A book to give children an awareness of the dangers lurking outside on the roads, on their bikes, near water, on building sites, etc. It is full of fun, puzzles and quizzes as well as being packed with information on how to stay safe.

THE ANIMAL QUIZ BOOK
Sally Kilroy

Why do crocodiles swallow stones? Which bird migrates the furthest? Can kangaroos swim? With over a million species, the animal kingdom provides a limitless source of fascinating questions. In this book Sally Kilroy has assembled a feast for enquiring minds – from domestic animals to dinosaurs, fish to footprints, reptiles to record breakers. Discover where creatures live, how they adapt to their conditions, the way they treat each other, the dangers they face – you'll be surprised how much you didn't know.